Lincoln: The English perspective

By: John Ruslan Clugg

IN MEMORY OF ABRAHAM LINCOLN.

Excessive admiration and praise for Lincoln was not
widespread until after he was killed.[1]

---

[1]Holzer, Harold. "What the Newspapers Said When
Lincoln Was Killed." Smithsonian.com. Smithsonian
Institution, March 1, 2015.

A Thesis

Submitted to the Department of History

The University of Tennessee

In Partial Fulfillment of the Requirements

for a Bachelor of Arts with Honors

May 2021

Adviser: Luke Harlow, Ph.D.

Table of Contents

Introduction

"Sic semper tyrannis"[2] was the Latin phrase yelled by Maryland native John Wilkes Booth as he assassinated President Lincoln on April 15, 1865. Lincoln was incredibly controversial, to the point of war. So, what changed to make him so loved by so many? His assassination.

In April 1861 a British anti-slavery society published an article about the new American president: "It may interest our [English] readers," the article began, "to learn something of the life and history of Mr. Abraham Lincoln, the first Republican President of the United States."[3] Immediately after his assassination in May 1865 the same paper reported, "In the present instance, our indignation is all the greater, our grief all profound,

---

[2] Linder, Doug. Diary Entry of John Wilkes Booth. Accessed April 22, 2021.

[3] "THE NEW AMERICAN PRESIDENT." *The anti-Slavery Monthly Reporter; Under the Sanction of British and Foreign anti-Slavery Society,* April 1, 1861. *Nineteenth Century UK Periodicals*: 21.

because Abraham Lincoln was not only a ruler, good, wise, and merciful, but the representative of a great principle, the champion of a great cause. To these he has fallen a martyr."[4] The first quote has a quiet tone, and merely identifies that there was a president far away who might be of some interest to some people. The second quote from the same paper wrote him a stirring eulogy, concluding with the claim that Lincoln was a martyr and a hero. This thesis is a story about that transformation, the dramatic change in President Lincoln's portrayed image in 1860s Great Britain.

Many Americans might remember the stories of President Lincoln from the U.S. school system; in the late nineteenth century there was also an abundance of interest in Lincoln among British

---

[4] "THE LATE ABRAHAM LINCOLN." *Anti-Slavery Monthly Reporter; Under the Sanction of the British and Foreign Anti-Slavery Society*, May 1, 1865.

people. It is noteworthy that the British newspaper took such an interest in Lincoln because at the time, many British people saw Great Britain as the world's superpower and a global empire. Why would an empire that size take an interest in an elected leader from across the Atlantic Ocean? In fact, Lincoln's actions and backstory inspired people globally. In the 1860s, the British press covered the presidency of Abraham Lincoln with avid interest. This thesis will explain the reasons behind that interest.

Richard Carwardine and Jay Sexton's edited volume of *The Global Lincoln* explored how Lincoln's image influenced people all over the world. This thesis will go further and identify the role of Lincoln's image. British culture in the 1860s, paying particular attention to his reception among the working classes and to the influence that his backstory had on public perception of him. Works such as *The Global Lincoln* help historians identify Lincoln's image worldwide, but this thesis will focus on the 1860s, and Lincoln's transformation from "honest Abe" to martyred hero in the eyes of the British. In the nineteenth century British people from all walks of life knew of Lincoln, and for a multitude of reasons, they developed different opinions about him. Social status influenced how people saw Lincoln, and the British working class developed a stronger interest in Lincoln than other social groups.

Newspapers provide primary source insights, and those insights are crucial when analyzing 1860s British viewpoints of President Lincoln. Analyzing newspapers from Great Britain at the time Lincoln was president helps to identify the reasons why certain British people developed figurative relationships and affection for a person with no direct or personal effect on them. Why was President Lincoln so popular with some people in Britain? Looking through an abundance of different types of British period newspapers will uncover the reasons for Lincoln's popularity. It can also help us better understand the role that Lincoln's assassination played in securing his public standing.

Chapter 1

Lincoln as a Global Figure

Renowned historian Richard Carwardine has edited the long-lasting global ramifications that contributed to President Lincoln's career. "Lincoln provided the perfect embodiment of the key features of 'modernity'," wrote Carwardine. "As a self-made man from humble origins, Lincoln stood for the dignity of labor; as statesman and war leader, he embraced the modernization of a national economy."[5] Lincoln was a relatable figure and in-step with the changing times that working-class Britons embraced. At the outbreak of the War Between the States, the British Empire was still the world hegemon. British papers were read globally

---

[5] Carwardine, Richard., and Jay Sexton. The Global Lincoln New York: Oxford University Press, 2011: 22-23.

and became the world standard and because of that, the British reception of Lincoln had a great deal of influence on his global reputation. As explained in *The Global Lincoln*:

> The 'British world-system' as it has recently been called, connected the world as never before…. The central, if often indirect, role played by British power in Lincoln's emergence as a global figure illustrates in microcosm the broader story of how the structures of the British Empire served as the launching pad for America's rise to superpowerdom.[6]

Although there are positives from the public opinion reflected in newspapers about Lincoln, others might see it as legitimizing colonization. Many made sweeping statements and generalizations regarding Lincoln because of their

---

[6] Carwardine, Richard., and Jay Sexton. The Global Lincoln New York: Oxford University Press, 2011: 16.

personal opinions. The reasons pushing the newspapers to publish such compliments of Lincoln are intriguing. I am going to analyze the effect Lincoln had on the global mood of ever-increasing liberalism, which led to more global support for emancipation. While no single person could amount to being the one true emancipator of all the enslaved peoples, it is important to analyze the good he did accomplish in cementing the already liberal people of the British working-class views from the newspaper's influence.

Eric Foner pursues Lincolns' global image in *The Fiery Trial*. The text speaks to his influence and lasting impact. During his lifetime, Lincoln was an inspirational figure, and his image and aura were both used by many. The sixteenth president was so much of a public figure that his words could be used to defend nearly any point of view. As Foner put it,

"In the last decade, his psychology, marriage, law career, political practices, literary style, racial attitudes, and every one of his major speeches have been subjected to minute examination."[7] Too many people have used Lincoln for too much, so Foner's goal is to break the enigma. As he writes, "My intent is to return Lincoln to his historical setting, tracing the evolution of his ideas in the context of the broad anti-slavery impulse and the unprecedented crisis the United States confronted during his adult life."[8] Foner spoke of how in a time of great crisis, Lincoln needed to be more neutral, please more people, and even gain more support. Seeing through the different lens's historians put on Lincoln to frame his speech exposes how it became

---

[7] Foner, Eric. The Fiery Trial : Abraham Lincoln and American Slavery 1st ed. New York: W.W. Norton, 2010: xv.
[8] Ibid. p. xvii.

obvious he was more opinionated than the average contemporary American might believe.

President Lincoln was anti-slavery, but he was not an abolitionist at the Wars' start. His anti-slavery views were held back from the main stage to avoid further controversies and potentially stop the South from succession. Through analyzing the impact post announcement, the Emancipation Proclamation made apparent that actions were not nearly as effective as remembered to be in conventional memories from textbooks. Emancipation was an entire process, not an event. The proclamation "freed" slaves in the southern states, but the Union did not have jurisdiction over them because the Confederacy recognized themselves as sovereign during the War. To avoid the border and only remaining slave states of Maryland, Delaware, Kentucky, and Missouri from joining the Confederacy, they were exempt from the proclamation, which meant even fewer potential slaves were freed. Slavery became the main reason why the Union continued to fight the War after it started, to obtain a moral high ground and have impeccable news propaganda supporting the efforts on the home front. Before slavery was a main issue in the war, and it was viewed as a War for Rights by many southern elites, some of the elites in England who sympathized with the South still had influence. Despite the Proclamations' lack of effect, it swayed the mood of many of the English commoners. They were inspired and now had a newfound feeling of sympathy for the enslaved peoples across the pond, and they felt they had to support the cause of the Union. President Lincoln who swore not to touch slavery where it already existed only "freed" slaves because it was a political move to keep Britain from joining the war and certainly achieving victory with the South. This was a political move which is important to analyze when looking into why so many people liked him. He knew what to do to keep people on his side. The summarized argument presented from Foner is that despite Lincolns' Good Samaritan views held later in his life, Lincoln grew into those views through exposure. His viewpoints were impacted by whom he encountered and where he traveled too.

Looking into Lincoln will identify that he strongly advocated for gradual emancipation, even after the war broke out to prevent the loss of the Border States to the Confederacy. Lincoln was quite mainstream, even colonization was considered normal as Foner identified, "Colonization was hardly a fringe movement."[9] Escaped slave and

---

[9] Foner, Eric. The Fiery Trial : Abraham Lincoln and American Slavery 1st ed. New York: W.W. Norton,

abolitionist Frederick Douglas even identified how "almost every respectable man approved of it."[10] Such an opinion from such a respected individual who achieved so much actually exposed the truth that most men, including Lincoln, were not radical or even abolitionists, despite being anti-slavery. Foner identifies how those around Lincoln swayed him. While debating Senator Stephen Douglas for the Republican ticket, Lincoln saw Henry Clay as a man with good opinions:

> Clay's outlook on slavery-condemnation of the institution and affirmation of the black's humanity coupled with the conviction that emancipation could only come gradually and should be linked with colonization-strongly affected Lincoln's.[11]

2010: 17.
[10] Ibid. p. 17.
[11] Ibid. p. 19.

Lincoln went so far as to say that he could quote Henry Clay and that could be his platform in entirety.

James McPherson, renowned author of the *Battle Cry of Freedom* analyzed the impact of Lincoln on the Confederate and other Southern states. Lincoln had to tread very carefully when dealing with the border states. Those other Southern States saw the Confederacy as their "Southern Brethren:"

> The governors of Kentucky, Tennessee, and Missouri not only refused to furnish any troops but sharply rebuffed Lincoln's requisition, finding it coercive and unconstitutional, a violation of the rights of their states and those of their southern brothers. Virginia, North Carolina, and Arkansas sent similar replies, while the governors of Maryland and Delaware remained ominously silent.[12]

The analysis identifies how the Mid-Southern states felt neutral, and if they felt their rights were violated, succession was an imminent threat. Those states never even answered Lincoln's call for troops and did not help the Union army retake the sovereign Confederate States of America.

Today, most people see America as the world hegemon. In the past, that was not the case. However, America was still of great concern to Britain because British curiosity toward America peaked. This peak can be attributed to the historical ties between Britain and their past colonies in the present-day America, but nonetheless, the British papers commented on American issues because the British interest was there. The article began with, "It may interest our [English] readers to learn

---

12 McPherson, James M., and James M. McPherson. The Illustrated Battle Cry of Freedom : the Civil War Era Oxford [U.K.] ;: Oxford University Press, 2003: 219.

something of the life and history of Mr. Abraham Lincoln, the first Republican President of the United States."[13] The London paper was perceived to be correct, many of the British people seemed to want to know about Lincoln. That was because he was so much different than anything they had ever experienced in their own government. Lincoln, previously viewed by elites as a commoner, who made his way to the Commander in Chief and Office of the Presidency and rarely lost the attention of our English-speaking friends. His organic and original past reminded working-class Britons that they too could make their dreams come true.

After Lincoln's assassination, people all over the world mourned. Following suit, England was no exception. From London 1865, "Few must

---

[13] "THE NEW AMERICAN PRESIDENT." *The anti-Slavery Monthly Reporter; Under the Sanction of British and Foreign anti-Slavery Society,* April 1, 1861. *Nineteenth Century UK Periodicals*: 21.

be the words, though deeply sad are our feelings, in which we record the death by an assassin's hand, of Abraham Lincoln."[14] It was truly astonishing the level of support our sixteenth president had overseas from the common masses, as *the anti-slavery monthly reporter* examined, "our grief all profound, because Abraham Lincoln was not only a ruler, good, wise, and merciful, but the representative of a great principle, the champion of a great cause."[15] Lincoln was a leader of the anti-slavery and abolition cause in the United States, and eventually globally, but once he was assassinated, he became a martyr. The victim of the heinous

---

[14] "THE LATE ABRAHAM LINCOLN." *Anti-Slavery Monthly Reporter; Under the Sanction of the British and Foreign Anti-Slavery Society*, May 1, 1865, 107+. *Nineteenth Century UK Periodicals* (accessed November 9, 2020): 11.

[15] "THE LATE ABRAHAM LINCOLN." *Anti-Slavery Monthly Reporter; Under the Sanction of the British and Foreign Anti-Slavery Society*, May 1, 1865, 107+. *Nineteenth Century UK Periodicals* (accessed November 9, 2020): 11.

murder was targeted as slavery itself, the institution so full of hatred, malice, and un-charitableness. Mr. Lincoln was well known, but his global reach spoke to how his qualities of universal respect led him to die a hero in the eyes of many.

On a Monday in January 1865, a journalist who wrote in the anti-Slavery Monthly Reporter; *Under the Sanction of the British and Foreign anti-Slavery Society* researched deep into the lives of Abraham Lincoln and his Vice President, Andrew Johnson. The article analyzed the backstory as to what the truth behind the backgrounds of Lincoln and Johnson really were. It most specifically points to the similarities of the predicaments of their upbringings that led them to do great things, despite circumstances, and to be able to credibly inspire the many people they touched and reached. "[Abraham Lincoln and Andrew Johnson] were born in the class of poor whites which slavery creates and preserves for its own convenience. Their early education was such as it accords to the children of this class."[16] Lincoln did not achieve most of his schooling once he became an adult who could push for the accomplishments of his own desires, and of course, move to a free state. Johnson never had any schooling, but in fact learned to read only when he left North Carolina for the almost fully free region of East Tennessee. They both never had a chance at being appointed to a slave state's legislature because they did not come from slaveholding families, and thus were not trusted to uphold the institution. The same newspaper identified that,

Abraham Lincoln entered Illinois a portionless, illiterate boy, earning the livelihood of his

---

[16] "LINCOLN AND JOHNSON." *Anti-Slavery Monthly Reporter; Under the Sanction of the British and Foreign Anti-Slavery Society*, January 2, 1865, 16+. *Nineteenth Century UK Periodicals*: 16.

widowed mother's family by the rudest and hardest manual labour, and, within twenty years thereafter, had become one of her foremost lawyers, and the acknowledged leader of the more intellectual of her two great political parties-conspicuous in her Legislature, her only Whig member of Congress, Whig candidate for Senatorial Elector, United-States Senator, Vice-President, and ultimately for President.[17]

The paper even continued to identify that each position was awarded without hesitation, because everyone who met future president Lincoln fell into believing he was truly a man of great things. The humble beginnings and steep impassable requirements that their birth disqualified them from was a reason why so many in Britain supported them as idols. Britain still operated with the ideals

---

[17] LINCOLN AND JOHNSON." *Anti-Slavery Monthly Reporter; Under the Sanction of the British and Foreign Anti-Slavery Society,* January 2, 1865, 16+. *Nineteenth Century UK Periodicals*: 16.

of the landed gentry holding power at the expense of the working class, so the fact that both Lincoln and Johnson accomplished winning the highest office of the country from poor uneducated backgrounds speaks to the reasons behind the many of the masses in Britain's attention and support. This is important to identify why so many in Britain developed a liking for him, the reasons why are the driving force behind this research. The conclusion from this publishing: Lincoln's humble beginnings lead him to receive some support from some disenfranchised groups across the pond who received little help from society to achieve success.

Abolition was not just an American phenomenon, but rather a global one. The global abolitionist phenomenon pressured American politics because of how firm anti-slavery viewpoints were. The London monthly reporter, a newspaper for the British and Foreign anti-Slavery society, made a piece depicting viewpoints after President Lincoln's assassination. After acknowledging the immense sadness for many of such an unexpected tragedy, the paper regarded John Wilkes Booth's crime as "unparalleled in atrocity."[18] Such powerful word choice was intentional because the paper was British, catering to the information desires of the many of the working-class British people, many of whom adored Lincoln and would see outspoken resentment as unacceptable to his reputation, and poor form regarding the post-assassination timing. The paper even refers to the attempt on his colleague, Seward, to be in poor taste as well. The significance of defaming those close to him was an

---

[18] GURNEY, SAMUEL, President, EDMUND STURGE, Chairman, and L. A. CHAMEROVZOW, Secretary. "ASSASSINATION OF PRESIDENT LINCOLN." *Anti-Slavery Monthly Reporter; Under the Sanction of the British and Foreign Anti-Slavery Society*, July 1, 1865, 158+. *Nineteenth Century UK Periodicals*: 10.

effort to question his judgement further by hesitating at whom he backs.

Social activist Henry Blackwell was running for office in England, and like many Englishmen, looked to the United States' very own Lincoln for inspiration for his platform. Blackwell knew he had to gain immense support from the British people to earn a seat in British Parliament, so to elevate his own status, he channeled Lincoln to gain support. In *The Women's Penny Paper*, Blackwell labeled Lincoln as a Pioneer Women Suffragist, and identified his platform where "man and women will be comrades and equals in society and in the home, in the Church, and in the State"[19] and frequently publicized his own platform in July 1898, decades after Lincoln's death. The fact that Lincoln was so

[19] Blackwell, Henry B. "ABRAHAM LINCOLN THE PIONEER WOMAN SUFFRAGIST." *Women's Penny Paper*, July 28, 1898. *Nineteenth Century UK Periodicals* (accessed November 9, 2020): 3-4.

inspirational to politicians that long after death speaks to the influence Lincoln had on politicians in England.

Rarely would the president be concerned with the wellbeing of such a disenfranchised group. Lincoln's care to many reflected the reasons why so many globally respected his character and willingness to listen, causing immense support worldwide for his causes. The analysis of the interpretation spoke directly to this analysis of an eagerness to listen. It was recorded, "To see the Great Father [Lincoln] had been the wish of their lives. The American Indians were poor, and required help."[20] The American Indians were one of the most overlooked, oppressed, and disenfranchised groups of American history, so the

---

[20] RHODES, ALBERT. "A REMINISCENCE OF ABRAHAM LINCOLN." *St. Nicholas Scribner's Illustrated Magazine for Girls and Boys*, November 1, 1876, 8+. *Nineteenth Century UK Periodicals*: 8.

fact that they found a United States government official to approve of was of immense importance. President Lincoln chose to listen to as many groups of people as he could, which is why he was more influential to more people. His ability to listen to others helped him gain the support and respect of many whom he listened to, including some of the non-influential peoples.

In 1881, published in the *St. Nicholas Scriber's illustrated Magazine for Girls and Boys* from London, England, the publication posted a copy of Lincoln's Gettysburg address. The point to notice, however, is that the magazine publication refers to Lincoln's speech as "immortal"[21] truly expressing how many of the English common boys and girls

---

[21] "IN our Treasure-Box of English Literature for June we gave you the immortal Gettysburg speech of Abraham Lincoln as it fell from the orator's lips*." *St. Nicholas Scribner's Illustrated Magazine for Girls and Boys*, September 1, 1881, 886+. *Nineteenth Century UK Periodicals* (accessed November 9, 2020): 73.

looked up to President Lincoln for his work in helping the "little people" gain hope to do big things, no matter the circumstances of their birth, a thought process ideology not quite universal in most of Europe for some time to come. The idea was not universal in most of Europe because many of the people lived in strict caste societies that were birthright. The Europeans had little exposure to the American way of life, and it showed, as the children in London felt like they could only accomplish so much, because at the time, many of them were restricted to the limits of their parents' success.

To help create the mythology behind Lincoln as a young child, rumors and stories surfaced to create the visions of "Honest Abe" many people know in modern times. One English paper participated in those story-telling goals and expressed opinions on why Lincoln gained the confidence of people everywhere. It was said that "everybody believed what Abraham Lincoln said was the exact truth, and so he became known as 'Honest Abe.'"[22] London paper, *The Chatterbox* went further to identify that Lincoln never spoke ill of anyone, and that it wasn't his genius, but his honesty and heart that made so many love him and his image.

Most every "hero" has a backstory. President Lincoln's had simple beginnings, and that was a contributing factor as to why he was as humble as he was. One 19th century London paper went into deep explanation, detailing the beginnings of Lincoln. Lincoln was illustrated as an American who was born poor, not even owning furniture more than stools. Lincoln was portrayed so impoverished

---

[22] "ABRAHAM LINCOLN." *Chatterbox*, April 14, 1883, 163. *Nineteenth Century UK Periodicals* (accessed November 9, 2020): 3.

that he did not teach himself to write with a pencil, as he could not afford one. It was written "he made his own pencil by putting one end of a stick into the fire until it was burnt to charcoal and wrote with this funny pencil on a flat piece of wood."[23] The London article continued to portray Lincoln's boyhood as simple to humanize him, which was the reasoning for so many worldwide to idolize him. President Lincoln was a champion of many in the working class, because he was portrayed as the working man. This connotation helped many working-class Americans find inspiration in Lincoln. He was portrayed to have lived the American dream, and that American Dream was known far beyond just America's boundaries and was renown by many in England as well.

---

[23] SMITH, SOPHIA L. "STORIES OF THE GOOD AND GREAT." *The Juvenile Companion and Sunday School Hive*, 1 Jan. 1888, p. 7+. *Nineteenth Century UK Periodicals*: 8.

Many people globally idolized our president, and that is partly because Britain did. The Great British Empire colonized most of the world's landmass and population, so in turn, what they identified as newsworthy is what all their worldwide subjects had an opportunity to believe as well. British Raj was under the control of the British Empire when Lincoln was the U.S. president. In the Kingdom of British Raj for example, the British honoring of Lincoln extended to the native local peoples, as they had no inspiring peoples themselves worthy of the front-page headlines. Decades after his death, the article published in British Raj points to Lincoln's crowning achievements, and the amount of influence he had over much of the world's population. The periodical stated that, "No one will deny that Abraham Lincoln is entitled to a place among the great rulers of mankind."[24] Such a bold statement without repercussions had to have been grounded in facts only becoming of a person whose rhetoric and actions spoke globally for the betterment of most of humanity. While many elites may not have idolized him, his fame grew and spread because of his connection with the common peoples of the world that united many of them in their efforts for the betterment of everyone, no matter their status.

Some people of a select but influential minority in Great Britain were seriously considering swaying Britain to come to the aid of the Confederacy because Great Britain was run by a small handful of land-owning aristocrats who dominated the political sphere. In this regard, much of the plantation parts of the American South were

---

[24] "ART. II.-ABRAHAM LINCOLN." *Calcutta Review*, April 1, 1892. *Nineteenth Century UK Periodicals* (accessed November 9, 2020): 14.

quite like the European standard from the bygone era, thus why some of the British elite wanted to come to the aid of the Confederacy. The thought of even some in Britain coming to the South's aid spurred Cotton Diplomacy, which entailed embargoing Europe's cotton supply to encourage support for the war. Despite the landed aristocracy holding a large share of control, there were large liberal forces coming out of the woodwork of working/labor-class England. Much of England has a sharp class divide. The sources in this thesis alone are proof that President Lincoln's speeches and writings were published in England. Much of the English population who were already sympathizing with the Republican Party platform saw Lincoln as their hero. He was seen as nearly emblematic for some of the British workers because of his policies that championed individual rights and freedoms.

Lincoln as an inspiration to the global working-class could only be established by those perceived positive actions made on their behalf. Much of the world was run by old elites, and Lincoln championed the argument to consider all possibilities. The reason his image became as influential as it did was because of the amount of people whom he inspired. There were people around the globe who looked to him as the shining example for the average person. The global impact is what inspired many to include him into so many myths and legends from all the nations, many which were engaged in change.

Richard Carwardine, editor of *The Global Lincoln* shed light on the world-wide effect of Lincoln, while analyzing the impact with Great Britain specifically. As explained, "Lincoln's international standing would burgeon over the next two generations, well into the 1920s at least; indeed, he would continue to be widely invoked throughout the twentieth century, in different places, at different times, for sundry purposes."[25] Such a viewpoint is helpful to understanding Lincolns' impact for "sundry" or many reasons which will cohesively identify the lasting effects. He later argued that Lincoln was "removed to the timeless sphere of mythical existence."[26] This identified how Lincoln was viewed by many which initiated the research to find out why. Each subsequent discussion regarding Lincoln recognized the global impact he had, specifically each of the discussions involving the working class. Carwardine saw Lincoln as the champion of the global working class; from his viewpoint Lincolns' international

[25] Carwardine, Richard., and Jay Sexton. The Global Lincoln New York: Oxford University Press, 2011: 5.
[26] Ibid. p. 5.

prestige never saw a downturn. Identifying one of the many written viewpoints,

> Outside the United States Lincoln would become a protean symbol. [...] This purposeful universalism or liberal nationalism spoke to a wide spectrum of political progressives abroad: socialists, radicals, and democrats, who combined nationalist aspirations with informal membership of a community dedicated to freeing the world from monarchical power, aristocratic privilege, and constrained popular rights.[27]

Such evidence identified how versatile of a symbol Lincoln was with such diverse groups of people.

When put together, these texts underline the main points regarding President Lincoln. President Lincoln was a man who will be remembered for all time; he was a world emblem for the working class

---

[27] Carwardine, Richard., and Jay Sexton. The Global Lincoln New York: Oxford University Press, 2011: 7.

and liberalism views. Lincoln was swayed by those around him and wanted to compromise to not let the border states succeed. Lincoln was considered a genius by many, and he knew how to manipulate his words into whatever everyone wanted to hear, his true talent was talking anyone and everyone into what he thought would be the best scenario for the country, not just himself. The Lincoln administration had to appease the northern American citizens, but his ability to gain international support was the most important. Europe's governments were not spectacularly interested in supporting the United States, but the European working and labor classes decided to once they read Lincoln's rhetoric which supported human rights and the rights of the lowest people in society sparked the commoners' support.

In 1881, published in the *St. Nicholas Scriber's illustrated Magazine for Girls and Boys* from London, England, the publication posted a copy of Lincoln's Gettysburg address. The point to notice, however, is that the magazine publication refers to Lincoln's speech as "immortal"[28] truly expressing how many of the English common boys and girls looked up to President Lincoln for his work in helping the "little people" gain hope to do big things, no matter the circumstances of their birth, a thought process ideology not quite universal in most of Europe for some time to come. The idea was not universal in most of Europe because many of the people lived in strict caste societies that were birthright. The Europeans had little exposure to the

---

[28] "IN our Treasure-Box of English Literature for June we gave you the immortal Gettysburg speech of Abraham Lincoln as it fell from the orator's lips*." *St. Nicholas Scribner's Illustrated Magazine for Girls and Boys*, September 1, 1881, 886+. *Nineteenth Century UK Periodicals* (accessed November 9, 2020): 73.

American way of life, and it showed, as the children in London felt like they could only accomplish so much, because at the time, many of them were restricted to the limits of their parents' success.

Eleven years after the assassination, in 1876, *the British magazine for boys and girls* described the national mood of Great Britain during the wake of his passing. The article, *A Reminiscence of Abraham Lincoln* identified shock. The death of the president was such a memorable and important moment that the average person, not just in America, but the world knew where they were when they knew Lincoln was killed! This is an association commonly paired with tragic events, as current examples include people knowing what they were doing when they found out about 9/11 or where they were when COVID-19 became real on a personal level. Many people all over the globe knew just how influential Lincoln was by influencing many global citizens with a passion for a positive change. This positive change included an ending for slavery and championing the common man. Lincoln, to hear the opinions of as many as possible who were willing to share, heard the opinions of a group not conventionally respected by the government of the United States, the American Indians. It was such a memorable moment for the people of the world that not just the United States officials, but also the President himself heard the disenfranchised, weak, and poor.

Even from a young age, many British Schoolchildren understood the basics of Lincoln, and the ensuing reasoning for why they should find value in certain aspects of life deemed important, such as school. Many of the schools in the British school system used Lincoln and his story to attempt to gain the attention and gratitude of the students. One teacher, as noted in The Child's Companion from London titled *an anxious pupil* noted a teachers use of the American President's humble beginnings and using that to make a connection for why the students should be grateful for school, implying not everyone has such an opportunity as influential and important as education. The school teacher's monologue to the students was recorded, after the story of Lincoln "you will say next time you feel cross because you have to go to school, instead of stopping at home to play, 'I'm sure I ought to be glad that I can go to school at all.'"[29] The newspaper continued by making in-depth arguments about why Lincoln should be and is a role model for the British schoolchildren. He only

---

[29] "AN ANXIOUS PUPIL." *The Child's Companion; or Sunday Scholar's Reward*, n.d., p. 170+. *Nineteenth Century UK Periodicals*: 170.

had a bible, so if the students have a library, there should be no handicap to their desire to learn. Lincoln's home was a log cabin. If the students have the privilege to study in a comfortable home, then there are no applicable arguments against the privilege of school simply because they were tired of it.

It has been identified that Lincoln's parents saved and sacrificed everything so that he could go to school. If the students come from more affluent backgrounds, there are no reasons to develop a distaste for school, because the opportunities for children brought up from good families are truly greater. The final major implication of Lincoln's childhood was he had no pencil, but a burnt stick and the ground, so writing became a challenge. He had no physical resources, so for the target audience, which was students in a proper British school, with supplies, there was no allowance to become disengaged with education. The main attempt of the article was to use Lincoln and his backstory to help the students identify that if Lincoln could do it with his miniscule resources, the students could certainly follow suit.

A famous British story published in the papers keenly named *From Ploughboy to President* exposes how truly humble Abraham Lincoln was portrayed and remembered as, and why that affected his international prestige in the eyes of many. The world-famous example the British try to recall and republish time and again was his perceived reaction when he won the Presidential nomination. It was said in common lore in England that, "Instead of delivering speeches, as many men would have done, all that Abraham Lincoln said was 'There is someone down at our house who would like to hear this. I'll go and tell her."[30] Lincoln was of course referring to his mother, and the kind act of caring more for her approval and sharing the news with her over the country speaks to the type of kindhearted person he was and who the British wanted their children to become. Was this accurate? That is not important. What is important, is why Lincoln was perceived that way, and the effects of that perception with many of the British people. He was portrayed as a loving son in Britain where many respect their elders. He was being marketed as British-similar to the British people by the British press through seemingly British actions, and that is why he was perceived as well as he was with such a large group of people.

---

[30] "FROM PLOUGHBOY TO PRESIDENT." *Little Folks: The Magazine for Boys and Girls; a Magazine for the Young*, n.d., 114+. *Nineteenth Century UK Periodicals*: 51.

Who is British? Yes, the English, Scots, Irish, and Welsh… But the British Empire incorporated so many more diverse populations than that. It is important to analyze non-English British viewpoints to note similarities. These similarities point to the influence London papers had, as what they published was projected to all corners of the worlds' largest empire. Lincoln was perceived as a humbled gentleman regarding his relationship with his mother. Regardless of what occurred which will never be exactly known, the level of his perceived appreciation was nearly unrivaled. This was another reason why many of the British people wished him to be a role model; his model of how to act was a perfect fit for the British children to use to inspire respect for their elders by mimicking Lincoln and his publicized relationship with his mother. Lincoln's famous statement was recorded by an

Australian newspaper, "All I am, or can be, I owe to my aged mother."[31] His sentiments to his mother were recorded as blatantly supportive, and thus the reason for the British to adore him to the level that they did. Britain views were global because of the global influence of the British Empire holistically, which stretched all the way to Australia. Many people in British society were delighted to learn that their children would have a positive role model to look up to. Another famous article from an Australian newspaper regarding Lincoln also included his mother. The Australian Journal from Melbourne expressed a Lincoln statement, which included his quote, "all I am, or can be, I owe to my angel mother."[32] The similarity is quite striking, but

---

[31] "TRIBUTES TO THE FAIR SEX." *Australian Journal*, September 1, 1898. *Nineteenth Century UK Periodicals*: 58.

[32] "THINGS SAID ABOUT WOMEN." *Australian Journal*, September 1, 1893, 55. *Nineteenth Century UK Periodicals*. 56.

the minute difference between the two is that he said aged mother the first time and angel mother the second. The former suggests his respect for elders, while the latter suggests his respect and devotion to divinity, another important trait that the British wanted to instill onto their youth. Holistically, many British parents wanted their children to idolize a man whose image portrays that of a gentleman.

The people of England, Wales, Northern Ireland, and Scotland were British. The size of the British Empire was imposing and tried to impose uniformity and a "Britishness", but the British People of all four countries were each incredibly different versions of British in their own way. Because of this, it is important to identify the Lincoln perspective of some non-English but still British peoples. Since Wales was British but, on the periphery, their mutual interest for Lincoln is important. Amongst so many differences, there was one similarity that we need to ask why it was so. In *The Global Lincoln*, Richard Carwardine edited the analysis to identify that the predicament of Wales was incredibly like the predicament of Lincoln. The text even identified highly important that, "Long before his assassination, he had become an iconic figure for many in Wales. For nonconformists, he was the very embodiment of their libertarian values."[33] The chapter continues to identify that Lincoln was almost "sanctified" because of his close ties to the American liberal ideas Wales so closely aligned with. Wales sided strictly with the abolitionist sentiment. It was even seen that, "No novel made a greater impact on Welsh-speaking Wales than did *Uncle Tom's Cabin*."[34] *Uncle Tom's*

---

[33] Carwardine, Richard., and Jay Sexton. The Global Lincoln New York: Oxford University Press, 2011: 139.
[34] Ibid. p. 140.

Cabin was a book, which depicted the horrors of slavery to an unbearable level. In Wales, the novel was immensely important to many for kindling political passions. "Most of the Welsh-language newspapers formed at this time [...] gave him full and favorable coverage. [...] From the start, Lincoln was claimed to embody Welsh values, such as social mobility, and the free ethic of the democratic-republican ideal."[35] The legend even identified him as Welsh, presenting an ancestry analogy to legitimize their newly desired heritage. Such a perspective is important to why Lincoln was so well received by so many Welsh. It comes down to being because the Welsh newspapers helped portrayed Lincoln as a man of them, which sat well with many of the Welsh.

---

[35] Ibid. p. 141.

Wales had begun its identity shift long before Lincoln, but because his policies so closely where portrayed as alongside Wales, his image was unofficially nominated by many of the Welsh people to be their inspirational hero. The namesake was even honored in newfound tradition, as "Lincoln became a recognized Welsh Christian name."[36] The Steelworkers' leader was even named Lincoln Evans. Many Welsh people viewed his "log cabin to President" backstory as inspirational motivation, and people who had any sort of self-improvement history felt compelled to make the connection, it almost legitimized claims of inner refinement.

Many of the Welsh people cared so deeply for Lincoln that some of them even established rumors to embellish their hopes. Questions of Mary

---

[36] Carwardine, Richard., and Jay Sexton. The Global Lincoln New York: Oxford University Press, 2011: 145.

Todd Lincoln's ancestry and his mother's came into light with the intention to push for relationships and ancestry connecting to Wales. "Through his mother, Nancy Hanks, it was believed that he could claim descent from medieval Welsh princes. His maternal grandmother was said to have come from Yspytty Ifan on the Caernarfonshire/Denbighshire border. The Scranton Welsh in 1909 referred hopefully to 'Our Welsh President.'"[37] The Welsh nationals wanted quite desperately to have Lincoln be, as they would like, one of their own. The people had their own Welsh heroes who fought for the United Kingdom, and who became the first Prince of Wales, but never had so many of them so readily clung to a foreign individual as a means of inspiration. The fact that a people so deep rooted in tradition and individual nationalism looked to an

---

[37] Ibid. 142.

international figure for inspiration suggest the truly immaculate characteristics of President Lincoln's image.

The love for Lincoln was not always without flaws. Many of the people loved his abolitionist ideals and hated the idea of anything less radical. When he became cautious regarding slavery, the support from many in Wales lessened. The support did not waiver however when he later in the war issued an executive order, the Emancipation Proclamation. "From then on, for almost all Welsh political and religious leaders, the Union cause had an unquestioned moral integrity." Post the Emancipation Proclamation, Wales strongly supported his unequivocal approach to the mutually agreed cause of freedom for the underdog; the slave who has no control, and Wales, who saw herself in the same light with no political efficacy in the United Kingdom.

Abraham Lincoln may have been an incredibly renowned inspiration by many of his constituents and followers in America, despite his heated controversies by many when he was president, but he was also incredibly inspirational for many around the globe. This is revealed by deep research into the world, specifically British, newspapers to see how the Europeans viewed our sixteenth President. In Britain, the working class and average people of the country adored him. In Wales, he was seen as the hero for abolition and the underdog, a predicament Wales viewed themselves in with regards to representation in the United Kingdom. The global perspective of Lincoln in the eyes of many was highly favorable, and that was in part because of his rhetoric, which focused strongly on the lowest common denominator, being portrayed to champion the labor class and even the enslaved people themselves. This new reputation Lincoln had built set him miles ahead of other leaders as a progressive inspiration. The best evidence for his appearance as a global hero can be found in the British newspapers from the period during his presidency, and how they responded after the assassination, glorifying him as a martyr and instituting him as a role model for future generations around the globe.

Chapter 2

British perspective, after assassination

"No martyr's cause has ever been stilled by an assassin's bullet." - Robert F. Kennedy (assassinated 1968).[38]

Many of the working-class British people in the nineteenth century felt distant from their government. The government was mostly elites who came to power from good families and ended up being out of touch with the general population of average working-class people. The mythology behind young President Lincoln's portrayal fascinated many Europeans, and British more than most because of the historical ties with the United

---

[38] Manchester, W.. "Robert F. Kennedy." Encyclopedia Britannica, Accessed 4/22/2021.

States. The idea of a national leader emerging from nowhere and dying a martyred hero was known but rare for the time. Socrates seizing influence, and then becoming a martyr after being charged with corrupting youth was one of the few previous examples. Many examples of martyrs existing after Lincoln identify and prove how Lincoln's assassination was the birth of his immortal fame with many. After analyzing the comparisons between British liberalism and elements of the United States Republican Party, President Lincoln received the support he did because he was portrayed as a man of the people to the people. This portrayal was consistent with the original elements of the United States Republican Party and British liberalism. Through interpreting British newspapers, the British perspective of President Lincoln shifted from being inspired by his origins to respecting his accomplishments. British people pre-assassination were obsessed with his early life and humble beginnings; by the time of Lincoln's assassination, the British people respected his policy and actions. Lincoln's induction to immortal status occurred because he was assassinated, and, as a result, martyred. Had he died of natural causes, his posthumous reputation might have been different. This chapter is a timeline of the story of change.

The similarity between British Liberalism and the US Republican Party are in the origins of both. With regards to British politics, "The Liberal Party was officially founded (1859) by a group of Whigs, Peelites, and radicals at Willis's rooms in St. James Street, London."[39] Since Elaine Hadley, author of *Living Liberalism*, identified mid-

---

[39] Hadley, Elaine. Living Liberalism : Practical Citizenship in Mid-Victorian Britain Chicago: University of Chicago Press, 2010.

Victorian British society, economics, and politics, she helped point to the creation of the British Liberal Party. The British Liberal Party and the US Republican Party both have roots stemming from the Whig Party, though not the same Whig Party. Many of the British Whig Party aristocrats left the Liberal Party to form what would eventually be the modern Conservative Party. That same founding history which explains the connection between British Liberals and US Republicans helped to spark the mutual liking for Abraham Lincoln.

The British government had many individuals present who were enlightened, but still not perfect, and as McDaniel put into words, "By 1855 [...] the enemies of democracy--monarchs, aristocrats, and their conservative defenders--still clung tightly to the reins of power in almost every state."[40] Democracy and slavery were mutually exclusive. If a nation was to be democratic, then they could not have slavery. Vice versa, if a nation was to uphold the institution of slavery, then democracy was nearly out of the question. The relationship between slavery and democracy in America and Western Europe was akin to the liking of the conflict between the working class and the landed aristocracy in Europe. In England specifically, that is why the outcome of the slavery question warranted attention and even the choosing of sides. The analysis stood that "liberal Englishmen now feared, on behalf of 'the Liberal Party throughout Europe,' that 'the one retrograde institution [slavery] in America is undermining the principle of progress, and fatally vitiating the noblest political system that the world ever saw.'"[41]

---

[40] McDaniel, W. Caleb. *The Problem of Democracy in the Age of Slavery: Garrisonian Abolitionists and Transatlantic Reform.* Baton Rouge: Louisiana State University Press, 2013.

Many British people took sides in the American

Civil War because those who did felt that the

outcome would affect democracy around the world.

The American experiment was on a path to devolve

into the bloodiest conflict America's soil has seen,

and the British had to decide where to stand.

The United States Republican Political Party

had an interesting birth. Because it was created as a

cutting-edge new party for the time, people

hesitated to join despite their general approval of

policies. "Some hesitated because of the high

mortality rates for third parties."[42] George Mayer,

author of *The Republican Party*, detailed an

intimate history of the Republican Party, makes an

important note that the professional politicians

---

[41] McDaniel, W. Caleb. *The Problem of Democracy in the Age of Slavery: Garrisonian Abolitionists and Transatlantic Reform*. Baton Rouge: Louisiana State University Press, 2013: 211.

[42] Mayer, George H. The Republican Party, 1854-1966. 2d ed. New York: Oxford University Press, 1967: 23.

would rather choose to have subordinate positions in established parties over a leadership role with a group whose future was uncertain.

Far from grand, in rural Wisconsin, (Ripon in 1854) the Republican Party was established for the working-class man, and in opposition to the Democrat Party which was in favor of the Kansas-Nebraska Act (1854). The photograph above depicts the humbled origins of the Republican Party's birthplace; it was quaint, quiet, yet about to be on the cusp of national political domination. A portion

---

43 "Little White Schoolhouse."

of the Democrat Party constituents supported the institution of slavery and its expansion west. A portion of the Republicans, seeking a free "republic", saw more progress to be made without the slave-holding establishment and other elites who controlled most of southern politics at the time. Those humble beginnings became the bedrock of attraction for many of the humbled Britons looking desperately to be heard by their own national government. The Republican Party's history stands in line with much of global liberalism's ideas such as liberty and freedom.

During the early years of the Republican Party, many of the men in charge had previously held power in the Whig Party. In the aftermath of the Whig downfall, the Republican Party seemed comparably good fortune to Whig politicians. That being the case, one can look at late Whig policy to identify potential early Republican platforms and values. The dominant pro-slavery Democrats stood as a formidable opposition. The new Republicans in Illinois needed a leader to help win against the pro-slavery Democrats, so many of them sought newfound inspiration in Abraham Lincoln because of his humbled beginnings. Lincoln began his political career as a Whig, and could have become influential, but the Party collapsed. Lincoln then had a choice to make to decide what party to join next, and he chose to seek refuge in the Republican Party. Lincoln's politics were tainted by Whig issues which were no longer important to the remaining parties. Lincoln and some of the other Whigs stole the Republican Party leadership spots from the original members, as none of the original Illinois Republicans were placed on the state ticket.[44]

---

[44] Mayer, George H. The Republican Party, 1854-1966. 2d ed. New York: Oxford University Press, 1967: Pg. 40.

Those initial elections nationwide had many opponents to the Democratic Party but would often take local or alternative names. This was because not all politicians who held Republican Party platform beliefs were comfortable with the label of being a Republican. The other parties that shifted into the Republican Party consisted of the Free-Soil Party, Liberty Party, and other local parties, as many of the Republicans desired to solve local problems and stay in touch with the people across America who suffered neglect from the government.

In reference to McDaniel, from Chapter one, via the lens of Transatlantic Abolitionism, Lincoln can be portrayed as the speaker of abolitionist rhetoric. This rhetoric can be hyper-scrutinized,

Garrisonians did not notice Lincoln's Peoria Speech, but its themes were indicative of a new era in antislavery politics; in the Republican

Party, Garrisonians would find increasing

evidence of what seemed like sympathy with

their own views, causing them to hope their

agitation was finally influencing politics.[45]

McDaniel furthers his argument that Lincoln

brought with him a new era of national anti-slavery

politics by continuing to show support for Lincoln's

new Republican Party. He identified that many of

the disunionists present at the time did not choose to

make an immense effort to oppose the Republicans.

He continued by claiming that those who opposed

"would instead 'wish well to the Republican

candidate as the best man, and will speak and act

accordingly.'"[46] Such a position shows how many

[45] McDaniel, W. Caleb. *The Problem of Democracy in the Age of Slavery: Garrisonian Abolitionists and Transatlantic Reform*. Baton Rouge: Louisiana State University Press, 2013: Pg. 211.

[46] McDaniel, W. Caleb. *The Problem of Democracy in the Age of Slavery: Garrisonian Abolitionists and Transatlantic Reform*. Baton Rouge: Louisiana State University Press, 2013: 211.

citizens from all corners of the nation would consciously choose to loyally support the Republican Party.

Another reason many why British commoners loved President Lincoln was because Lincoln got to the point, said what he needed to say, and eliminated fluff. There was typically no guessing with Lincoln; rather, he was portrayed as someone who made his platform clear as could be. When the speeches of the Confederate States of America President Jefferson Davis, and United States of America President Abraham Lincoln were compared, the study results were on par with expectations. Davis composed phenomenal statements and speeches, whilst using impeccable language and rhetoric. Rustically portrayed Lincoln however did not follow suit. As identified in EUROPE AND AMERICA from 1865,

Mr. Lincoln's speech takes no such lofty or heroic ground; nor was it necessary that he should. He nevertheless speaks sensibly and to the purpose; declares the end of the rebellion to be close at hand from the exhaustion of the South in men; and administers a caustic rub on the dislocated back of slavery, by declaring that if one-fourth of the Southern slaves fight and are willing to fight for the prolonged enslavement of the other three-fourths, slavery as an institution will find its best justification in so strange and abnormal a fact.[47]

President Jefferson Davis of the Confederate States currently was charismatic and emphatically asserting that Richmond, the Capital of the Confederacy, was never in peril of invasion, nor even close to the later inevitable surrender of the short-lasting sovereign and independent Country. A

[47] "EUROPE AND AMERICA." *The Friend of India*, May 4, 1865, 521+. *Nineteenth Century UK Periodicals.*

British working-class person would typically appreciate the transparent, honest, and straight forward speaker. There was immense support for British heroes. Much later, Sir Winston Churchill and Margret Thatcher who championed patriotism in the face of opposition became some of the most favorite politicians because of their speeches. Speeches mean so much to many British citizens That same Briton would identify the speech patterns of Lincoln as more easily understood than his adversary, President Davis, who catered to his constituents of the elite slavocracy, who of course naturally preferred systematically complex language and even also supported lies to the less intellectually gifted masses to maintain support.

The Anti-Slavery Monthly Reporter in London titled the front page THE LATE ABRAHAM LINCOLN after his assassination. A close reading proved that the assassination was a contributing factor in his status in the memories of many. From May 1865, "In the present instance, our indignation is all the greater, our grief all profound, because Abraham Lincoln was not only a ruler, good, wise, and merciful, but the representative of a great principle, the champion of a great cause. To these he has fallen a martyr."[48] The paper identified him as a martyr, and that is because he was labeled as more than just an influential ruler; he was portrayed as a champion of the cause of freedoms and civil rights. When a person labeled as a champion of anything is murdered, it is justification in the eyes of many to label that person as a martyred hero.

---

[48] "THE LATE ABRAHAM LINCOLN." *Anti-Slavery Monthly Reporter; Under the Sanction of the British and Foreign Anti-Slavery Society*, May 1, 1865.

More paper headings from the London Anti-Slavery Reporter include THE NEW PRESIDENT also from May 1865. The paper put a spotlight on newly sworn-in President Johnson. The article doubts the abilities of Johnson because the writers believed there was no one who could fill the shoes of President Lincoln. "For the affairs of a great nation, and the special destinies of 4,000,000 people, in whose welfare we are deeply interested, and who have scarcely been released from bondage, are committed to his hands."[49] The writing identified "his hands" as Johnson's hands, the new caretaker for all citizens and people. The article claimed that Lincoln's action to free the slaves was Lincoln's defining moment which led so many to become inspired by him as a person, and his image.

---

[49] "THE NEW PRESIDENT." *Anti-Slavery Monthly Reporter; Under the Sanction of the British and Foreign Anti-Slavery Society*, May 1, 1865.

The article also proves there was some doubt from a great number of men and women that Johnson would live up to the looming task. The details from the writer shifting responsibility to Johnson proves that many of the people of Great Britain saw the death of Lincoln as the death of the image of unrelentless progress at any cost, including war, the War of Northern Aggression. They had lower expectations for anyone else, including newly sworn-in President Johnson.

One British lord expressed sympathy. The sympathy from some British elites suggests that the assassination brought many more followers to Lincoln and his portrayed glorified image, as opposed to if he died peacefully as just another American liberal policy president. The Morning news from May, 1865, included a statement from the House of Lords, "The Noble lord expects however, to be sufficiently convalescent to attend in his place this evening, and move an address to the Crown, expressive of the horror and indignation with which the House has heard of the assassination of President Lincoln."[50] Lincoln's assassination and becoming of a martyr gained more movement for the liberal cause globally than he could have accomplished alive as the US president solely.

The Belfast Morning News also expressed more sympathy for President Lincoln after his death in May 1865, as the paper reflected that "there was great sympathy in the British provinces for Lincoln."[51] The source explained in further detail that there were Lincoln memorial services in the United Kingdom, implying an abundance of grief from the Britons themselves. Some of those

---

[50] "The Morning News." *Belfast Morning News*, May 1, 1865, 3. *British Library Newspapers.*
[51] "Latest Telegrams." *Belfast Morning News*, May 1, 1865, 3. *British Library Newspapers.*

meetings went so far as to include funeral ceremonies.

In May 1865, included in *ENGLISH SYMPATHY WITH THE UNITED STATES*, is the reminder that the United States and England shared an uncommonly close related heritage with each other's histories being quite intertwined at the founding of the United States. The paper continued to identify how "President Lincoln was only the chief of a foreign State, and of a State with which we were not infrequently in diplomatic or political collision."[52] Important because the United States and British governments shared political collision, and thus a mutual feeling for each other's heads of state. The source also continues to explain how the whole viewpoint from British parliament was an

---

[52] "ENGLISH SYMPATHY WITH THE UNITED STATES." *Belfast News-Letter*, May 1, 1865. *British Library Newspapers.*

expression of "sincere and unaffected sympathy."[53] Viewpoints are shared much easier with groups who share common ground, and with ground as common as the histories between the United States and Britain, there was ample room in both countries for sorrow after Lincoln's death.

Another document from the United Kingdom, which details the murder of President Lincoln proves how "the cause" of abolition could not falter because Lincoln was assassinated. "And yet the cause must win, not only because Providence governs as well as reigns - though events like the one we deplore force even politicians to recall the single certainty of politics - not only because a cause never hangs upon a single life, but because of the special circumstances of this individual case."[54] The special circumstance the

---

[53] Ibid.

[54] "MURDER OF PRESIDENT LINCOLN." *Birmingham*

paper refers to is President Lincoln and the relationship he had with civil rights and abolition. More attention was drawn to Lincoln's death because since he was portrayed so commonly as a champion of a cause who was assassinated, many were worried the cause would falter or even lose traction. The paper identified that it would not be the case, as Lincoln's cause was so well established under his influence.

Again, in May 1865 immediately after the assassination, the article titled, *Further Particulars of the Murder of Mr. Lincoln* explained the British interpretation. Since he was brutally murdered, front-page articles and coverage was given. The article depicts exact specifications to the assassination including when Lincoln did what leading up to the event.[55] Such detail was only

---

Daily Post, May 1, 1865. *British Library Newspapers.*
[55] "Further Particulars of the Murder of Mr. Lincoln." *Belfast*

offered because the readers found his death fascinating. Lincoln's assassination helped fuel his influence globally because of the common man's interest with the global events.

One British newspaper identifies the Civil War as the American War. CANADA AND THE AMERICAN WAR explained how President Lincoln perished by the hands of an assassin. The paper pointed out how "In the removal of Lincoln the States have lost 'the great pillar that upholds the commonwealth"[56] The paper examines that the "American War" concluded, as well as the work of Lincoln who was a "pillar" who held up the United States. The image of this Lincoln pillar, as portrayed, was such a strong one, that when he was assassinated, he left a void because no one prepared

---

Morning News, May 1, 1865, 4. *British Library.*

[56] "CANADA AND THE AMERICAN WAR." *Birmingham Daily Post*, May 1, 1865. *British Library Newspapers.*

to fill his shoes. Many of the British saw President

Lincoln as a fallen hero for this cause once he was

assassinated.

Another London paper included the

sentiments of mourning after Lincoln's death. The

publicity of Lincoln's death across Britain is

certainly why many of the British people felt agony

for his loss. One paper headline circa 1865 certainly

pointed out that "a miscreant - whom we sincerely

trust may prove to be a maniac [John Wilkes Booth]

-shot the unsuspecting patriot [President Lincoln]

through the brain."[57] The newspaper labeled John

Wilkes Booth, not yet identified at the time of

publication, as a "maniac" and referred to Lincoln

as a "patriot", which communicates a clear point of

view. The paper did not take the reserved path of

---

[57] "ASSASSINATION OF PRESIDENT
LINCOLN." *Anti-Slavery Monthly Reporter; Under
the Sanction of the British and Foreign Anti-Slavery
Society*, May 1, 1865.

just facts of who shot who but took the side of

Lincoln and placed value claims on members of the

narrative because Lincoln was the victim. That

taking of sides extended to calling Booth and

Lincoln names, as if the sympathies were not

already clear.

During the period of Gladstonian

Liberalism, the sincerity of an orator's speech was

valued highly by many. Regarding conviction, "It

seems likely that the growing activism of

government in eighteenth century America and

nineteenth-century Britain contributes to sincerity's

authenticating prowess because policy-driven

government posits a motive force that is most often

traced back to the populace through the candidate

form."[58] Hadley further identified how Victorian

---

[58] Hadley, Elaine. *Living Liberalism: Practical Citizenship in
     Mid-Victorian Britain*. Chicago: University of
     Chicago Press, 2010: 310.

Liberalism was conventionally skeptical of democratic principles. Gladstone was portrayed as a man of the people, and was no longer the Liberal Party leader, but still an influential and favorite liberal for many of the British. It is interesting to note the relationship both Gladstone and Lincoln had with the British working-class because of their similarities. Both born in 1809, Gladstone and Lincoln were the same age. They also had some similar goals, and political ideologies. The similarities between Gladstone and Lincoln are numerous and shed light on their comparable platforms. After Lincoln's death, Gladstone took over the transatlantic Liberal Party movement. Lincoln's influence after assassination never faded with many. His martyrdom kept him incredibly relevant with many more for longer. In a political cartoon, William Gladstone was standing at the base of a tree watching a tall man cut it down with an axe.[59] The man with the axe is Abraham Lincoln, and a reader can infer the following message: William Gladstone watched as Abraham Lincoln made liberal politics gain sweeping victories in America, and after Lincoln could do no more, Gladstone picked up the axe and kept swinging until his death as well. The tree represented the oppression of the working-class because of how thick it was, and Gladstone's drive to pick up the axe represented the continuity of championing the working-class. The brotherhood between the two men was astonishing to many, and their physically distant, but similar mind relationship shows the importance which was transatlantic liberalism on the global scale. Lincoln was the champion of

---

[59] Hadley, Elaine. *Living Liberalism: Practical Citizenship in Mid-Victorian Britain*. Chicago: University of Chicago Press, 2010: 338.

liberal politics in America, but on the global world stage he was another influencer who came and went. The reasons that Lincoln's image inspired the masses to get on board with new ideas were grounded in his martyrdom. He became a bigger liberal policy maker in history by signing the Thirteenth, Fourteenth, and Fifteenth Amendments into laws. At least in America, more people would be familiar with the name Lincoln than with Gladstone, despite Gladstone working much longer, but not having a brutal assassination as an end to lead to martyrdom.

When identifying republicanism and liberalism, it is crucial not to think of who supports or denies rights. As E. F. Biagini argued, "for the real questions in the history of both republicanism and liberalism are not about 'positive' or 'negative' liberty, but about *who* should enjoy such liberties in the first place."[60] Controversy can derive from disagreement about prominent actions or people. In that instance, when identifying that no Party or organization in the United States was against liberty, it was crucial to understand what each platform stood for to identify whom they thought deserved those liberties in question.

The newly created Republican Party cry was chanted by the delegates, "Free Soil, Free Labor, Free Speech, Free Men."[61] These initial ideals of many in the Republican Party stood for enlightened freedom for the common man, and an end to the establishment of Democrat-elite domination, as experienced in the South. These Republican values were highly attractive to many of

---

[60] E.F. Biagini (2003) Neo-roman liberalism: "republican" values and British liberalism, ca. 1860–1875, History of European Ideas, 29:1, 55-72.

[61] Mayer, George H. The Republican Party, 1854-1966. 2d ed. New York: Oxford University Press, 1967: Pg. 44.

the people in Great Britain, who also sought more

equal opportunities for success and to flourish as

individuals. Evidence is present in nineteenth

century newspapers. The Free-Soil Doctrine became

the Republican platform.[62] The Doctrine established

that slavery was not to be touched where it

previously existed, but that the expansion into the

territories was wrong. Many in the Republican Party

took the idea that slavery would just naturally die

out. Many of the English people took note of these

developments. The Slavocracy of the American

South were Plantation owners who held most of the

land dominated local politics was quite like the

situation in Great Britain where a minority of elite

landed aristocracy held a vast majority of power.

The desire for change in Britain, by many British

---

[62] Myers, William Starr. The Republican Party, a
History. Rev. ed. with additions. New York: The
Century co., 1931: 79.

working-class people is what motivated the

inspiration behind favoring the influence and

history of President Lincoln.

Many of the British people would like

images of Lincoln, which appeared in papers. He

was always portrayed as a humbled man, a man

with whom the working class of Britain could relate

to. In one cartoon, Lincoln arrived alongside

established men of the time and was surrounded by

those men in formal clothing, including cutaway

tails, waistcoats, and of course a gentleman's cravat,

or bow tie.[63]

---

[63] SCHNAPPER, M. B. *GRAND OLD PARTY: the First*
Hundred Years of the Republican Party. Washington,
D.C.: Public Affairs Press, 1955: 49.

"TAKING THE STUMP" OR STEPHEN IN SEARCH OF HIS MOTHER.

Lincoln was portrayed as rustic and was clad in a loose white shirt with an open collar. Such was not the signal of refinement, respectability, or any form of class advancement. He even was carrying an axe during a time when associating tools and work was unbecoming of a gentleman when being a gentleman meant everything to many. The axe represented his perceived difference from the elites, and the permanence in its presence represents the idea that the elites would never forget his roots and difference. This conglomerate of evidence was of course implication enough that the established gentlemen did not welcome him to their game of politics. His portrayal before his assassination was not always optimal, and that is because he had not become a martyr yet. When he became a martyr, then he changed from an inspiration to becoming immortalized as a champion of liberalism, progressivism, and change.

It is important to identify the relationship between the British people and the American Civil War as a whole. Many of the British people were already familiar with sectionalism and regional differences and issues, so Abraham Lincoln's opinions slid into pre-existing expectations and already grasped conflicts. President Abraham Lincoln's connection with many of the British people was grounded in similar backgrounds and modern ideas. After analyzing the position of Lord Palmerston's foreign and domestic policy from

Anthony Wood's *Nineteenth Century Britain 1815-1914*, much of Britain was divided. The division was caused by many factors. One of the main factors was class. "The [British] upper classes naturally preferred the Southern gentleman to the hard-headed Yankee businessman. British shippers saw a chance of capturing Southern carrying trade, which had been in the hands of the Northerners. British manufacturers knew that the Southerners hated tariffs and hoped that the new Confederacy might mean an extension of the area of free trade."[64] Furthering the perceived class divide was the British common worker's viewpoint. "It was the British working class of the industrial regions who most wholeheartedly supported the North."[65] The reason behind Union and Northern sympathies from

---

[64] Wood, Anthony. *Nineteenth Century Britain 1815 - 1914*. London: Longman, 1984: 241.

[65] Wood, Anthony. *Nineteenth Century Britain 1815 - 1914*. London: Longman, 1984: 241.

British commoners lay with the numerous peoples in the British working class. British immigrants who made it to the industrialized North, with more opportunities for success and security attracted the affections of British people back in England who saw Lincoln as the savior of their fellow brethren, coinciding with many of the British workers in England suffering the same harsh reality. Much of Britain was divided with the outbreak of the war, and thus frustrated with deeply ingrained disagreement. Lord Palmerston was the British Prime Minister and dominated British foreign policy from 1830 through 1865. When identifying Lord Palmerston's foreign policy, it is clear that; "British opinion was utterly divided. There was no liking for the slavery that the southerners hoped to protect. But Lincoln had made it clear that slavery was not the issue."[66] It was revealed later that

Lincoln's 'free soil' policy simply contained no extension of slavery, and that the War Between the States was about preserving the Union. The text continued by identifying that those as famous as William Gladstone proclaimed that "There is no doubt that Jefferson Davis, and other leaders of the South, have made an Army. [...] They have made a nation."[67] This comment helped the American Minister in London to believe that Britain was going to support the Confederate States of America, which President Lincoln never believed sovereign and legitimate. Those British working class, supporters of the United States, were the reason why some British opinion became more neutral, especially after Lincoln "freed" the slaves with the Emancipation Proclamation and turned the War of

---

[66] Ibid. p. 240.
[67] Ibid. p. 241.

Southern Independence into a war which had much more to do with slavery than originally intended.

Many of the British people looked at the US Republican Party as the stronghold for liberalism and Liberal politics in the United States. Lincoln had portrayed humble beginnings like the working-class Britons. He then became the head of the US Republican Party. The combination of the US Republican Party being a liberal stronghold in America, and working-class Britons being liberal sparked much of British approval, support, and even inspiration from President Lincoln's portrayed image across the pond.

Understanding the reasons behind the newly established relationship of the British people and President Lincoln is intriguing. It is important to note any similarities or differences between the interpretations of Lincoln before and after his assassination. Conventionally, when a person who is labeled as a head of a cause or movement is assassinated, they almost certainly become a martyr. Did the British working class who for so long appreciated Lincoln see him any different after John Wilkes Booth ended the Lincoln Presidency? It is compelling to say yes because Lincoln was immortalized after his death. Through analyzing British newspapers immediately after Lincoln's assassination, many of the British idolized him because of his martyrdom.

Conclusion

"The tyrant dies and his rule is over, the martyr dies
and his rule begins." - Søren Kierkegaard, widely considered
the first existentialist philosopher.[68]

Assassination has been proven as means to
make someone glorified after death. Many of the
great inspirational heroes from different cultures in
history, including Gandhi, Dr. Martin Luther King
Jr., and even Lord Mountbatten all accomplished a
great deal while they were alive, but assassination
allowed them to be remembered as a victim of
violence and savagery in their goals of building a
more peaceful world or a civilized order. Lincoln
had these same goals of building a more perfect
Union, and his efforts too lasted only until he was

---

[68] "Søren Kierkegaard." Encyclopedia Britannica.
Encyclopedia Britannica, inc., March 24, 2021.

assassinated. Gandhi had dreams of an independent India, Dr. King had dreams of an equal society, and Lord Mountbatten had his quest for expanding the influence of progress, order, and civilization. Gandhi was shot by an opposing extremist, Dr. King was also shot by an extremist who opposed King's beliefs, and Lord Mountbatten was bombed and gruesomely murdered with his family by the irrational and savage Irish Republican Army.

The reason why Abraham Lincoln was so well received in Britain and the world was because he was brutally killed in a manner so publicly and savage that it is impossible not to sympathize with him, despite the many potential disagreements, of which they were from the entire globe. President Abraham Lincoln was perhaps the most controversial President America has ever had, to the literal breaking point, yet his assassination immortalized his positive attributes and

accomplishments worldwide. This is made apparent

when analyzing British nineteenth century

newspapers to understand why the working-class

Britain cherished the perceived image of President

Lincoln.

Bibliography

"ABRAHAM LINCOLN." *Chatterbox*, April 14, 1883, 163.

> *Nineteenth Century UK Periodicals* (accessed
> November 9, 2020)

"AN ANXIOUS PUPIL." *The Child's Companion; or Sunday
> Scholar's Reward*, n.d., p. 170+. *Nineteenth Century
> UK Periodicals*

"ART. II.-ABRAHAM LINCOLN." *Calcutta Review*, April 1,
> 1892. *Nineteenth Century UK Periodicals* (accessed
> November 9, 2020).

"ASSASSINATION OF PRESIDENT LINCOLN." *Anti-
> Slavery Monthly Reporter; Under the Sanction of the
> British and Foreign Anti-Slavery Society*, May 1,
> 1865

Blackwell, Henry B. "ABRAHAM LINCOLN THE
> PIONEER WOMAN SUFFRAGIST." *Women's
> Penny Paper*, July 28, 1898. *Nineteenth Century UK
> Periodicals* (accessed November 9, 2020).

"CANADA AND THE AMERICAN WAR." *Birmingham
> Daily Post*, May 1, 1865. *British Library Newspapers*
> (accessed March 1, 2021).

Carwardine, Richard., and Jay Sexton. The Global Lincoln

    New York: Oxford University Press, 2011

E.F. Biagini (2003) Neo-roman liberalism: "republican"

    values and British liberalism, ca. 1860–1875, History

    of European Ideas, 29:1, [Pg. 55-72]

"ENGLISH SYMPATHY WITH THE UNITED STATES."

    Belfast News-Letter, May 1, 1865. *British Library*

    Newspapers

"EUROPE AND AMERICA." *The Friend of India*, May 4,

    1865, 521+. *Nineteenth Century UK Periodicals*

Foner, Eric. The Fiery Trial : Abraham Lincoln and American

    Slavery 1st ed. New York: W.W. Norton, 2010.

"Further Particulars of the Murder of Mr. Lincoln." *Belfast*

    Morning News, May 1, 1865, 4. *British Library*

"FROM PLOUGHBOY TO PRESIDENT." *Little Folks: The*

    Magazine for Boys and Girls; a Magazine for the

    Young, n.d., 114+. *Nineteenth Century UK*

    Periodicals

GURNEY, SAMUEL, President, EDMUND STURGE,

    Chairman, and L. A. CHAMEROVZOW, Secretary.

    "ASSASSINATION OF PRESIDENT LINCOLN."

    Anti-Slavery Monthly Reporter; Under the Sanction

of the British and Foreign Anti-Slavery Society, July 1, 1865, 158+. *Nineteenth Century UK Periodicals*

Hadley, Elaine. *Living Liberalism: Practical Citizenship in Mid-Victorian Britain*. Chicago: University of Chicago Press, 2010.

Holzer, Harold. "What the Newspapers Said When Lincoln Was Killed." Smithsonian.com. Smithsonian Institution, March 1, 2015.

"IN our Treasure-Box of English Literature for June we gave you the immortal Gettysburg speech of Abraham Lincoln as it fell from the orator's lips*." *St. Nicholas Scribner's Illustrated Magazine for Girls and Boys*, September 1, 1881, 886+. *Nineteenth Century UK Periodicals* (accessed November 9, 2020).

"Latest Telegrams." *Belfast Morning News*, May 1, 1865, 3. *British Library Newspapers*

"LINCOLN AND JOHNSON." *Anti-Slavery Monthly Reporter; Under the Sanction of the British and Foreign Anti-Slavery Society*, January 2, 1865, 16+. *Nineteenth Century UK Periodicals*

Linder, Doug. Diary Entry of John Wilkes Booth. Accessed
    April 22, 2021.

"Little White Schoolhouse." Wikipedia. Wikimedia
    Foundation, February 7, 2021.

Manchester, W.. "Robert F. Kennedy." Encyclopedia
    Britannica, Accessed 4/22/2021.

Mayer, George H. The Republican Party, 1854-1966. 2d ed.
    New York: Oxford University Press, 1967.

McDaniel, W. Caleb. *The Problem of Democracy in the Age of*
    Slavery: Garrisonian Abolitionists and Transatlantic
    Reform. Baton Rouge: Louisiana State University
    Press, 2013.

McPherson, James M., and James M. McPherson. The
    Illustrated Battle Cry of Freedom : the Civil War Era
    Oxford [U.K.] ;: Oxford University Press, 2003.

"MURDER OF PRESIDENT LINCOLN." *Birmingham Daily*
    Post, May 1, 1865. *British Library Newspapers*

Myers, William Starr. The Republican Party, a History. Rev.
    ed. with additions. New York: The Century co., 1931.

SCHNAPPER, M. B. *GRAND OLD PARTY: the First*
    Hundred Years of the Republican Party. Washington,
    D.C.: Public Affairs Press, 1955.

"Søren Kierkegaard." Encyclopedia Britannica. Encyclopedia
   Britannica, inc., March 24, 2021.

"THE LATE ABRAHAM LINCOLN." *Anti-Slavery Monthly*
   Reporter; Under the Sanction of the British and
   Foreign Anti-Slavery Society, May 1, 1865, 107+.
   Nineteenth Century UK Periodicals (accessed
   November 9, 2020).

"The Morning News." *Belfast Morning News*, May 1, 1865, 3.
   British Library Newspapers

"THE NEW AMERICAN PRESIDENT." *The anti-Slavery*
   Monthly Reporter; Under the Sanction of British and
   Foreign anti-Slavery Society, April 1, 1861.
   Nineteenth Century UK Periodicals

"THE NEW PRESIDENT." *Anti-Slavery Monthly Reporter;*
   Under the Sanction of the British and Foreign Anti-
   Slavery Society, May 1, 1865

"THINGS SAID ABOUT WOMEN." *Australian Journal*,
   September 1, 1893, 55. *Nineteenth Century UK*
   Periodicals

"TRIBUTES TO THE FAIR SEX." *Australian Journal*,
   September 1, 1898. *Nineteenth Century UK*
   Periodicals

Wood, Anthony. *Nineteenth Century Britain 1815 - 1914.*

London: Longman, 1984.

Made in the USA
Monee, IL
15 September 2021